A WALK
WITH CHARLES
DICKENS
& OTHER POEMS

Bridget Nolan

A Walk with Charles Dickens and Other Poems

Published by The Conrad Press in the United Kingdom 2018

Tel: +44(0)1227 472 874
www.theconradpress.com
info@theconradpress.com

ISBN 978-1-911546-23-8

Typesetting and Cover Design by:
Charlotte Mouncey, www.bookstyle.co.uk

The Conrad Press logo was designed by Maria Priestley.

Printed and bound in Great Britain by Clays Ltd, St Ives plc

A Walk with Charles Dickens

Including Poems for Niamh

with all good wishes,

[signature]

For my children and their children.

Contents

A Walk with Charles Dickens

I took a walk with Charles Dickens last night,
It was dark and my chest felt quite tight.
'Don't worry,' he said, 'old Marley is dead,
There's nothing to give you a fright.'

I couldn't shake off my dread sense of fear,
Magwitch, I felt sure, was skulking quite near.
'That convict,' he said, 'is certainly dead,
For he's been quiet and gone this whole year.'

From the High Street we turned into Crow Lane,
We reached Satis House and Charles lifted his cane.
'That, my dear,' he said, 'is where she lay dead,
After years of poison and pain.'

Just then, in The Vines, I thought I saw Pip
With his arm held loosely on Estella's hip.
CD saw them too and I watched,
As a quiver danced on his lip.

At the castle I asked him about Edwin Drood.
'My dear,' he sighed, 'I'm not really in the mood
To reflect on his fate.'
And I knew to persist would seem rude.

We strolled slowly to the Bull Inn,
Where quite a commotion was heard from within.
'I do hope Pickwick is not in some scrape,'
Mr Dickens said with a sly grin.

We paused outside old Guildhall Court,
Where Dickens seemed lost in deep thought.
'In there,' he whispered, 'fates are decided
And many hard lessons are taught.'

At Eastgate House we boarded a carriage,
Traversed the High Street and went over the bridge
To Cooling marshes, where the fog grew thick.
It was here where young Pip showed such courage.

Dickens led me to the chalet at Gad's Hill Place
And I'll never forget the look on his jocular face;
All those people his famed works presented,
Play their part in our great human race.

I glimpsed his literary genius,
Included today on every syllabus.
I felt the energy in that chalet,
My privilege was wondrous.

I took a walk with Charles Dickens last night,
We wandered around as the dark turned to light.
'I must go now,' he smiled, kissed my trembling hand,
And with that he vanished from sight.

2017

The Royal Military Canal

We choose to journey upon our trusty
Old bikes, somewhat rickety and rusty.
The cool water reflects the pink blue sky
Like a huge undiscovered butterfly.
Yellow water lilies float serenely
And bees explore the dead nettles keenly.
Formed of the sweat of men in history,
Carrying lives and times of mystery.
Fishermen sit tranquil and full of hope.
The crows circle round and the mad hares lope.
This is us. This is real. We stop and steal
A peep at the ducklings. Trying to heal
The hole in our world. This gives us respite.
These things, we wanted to show her, and more.
The hole in our world is constantly sore.
The water winds on through modernity,
We cycle on through our solemnity.
Then we reach the path that borders the zoo
And we hear the squeals of the children who
Spot the giraffes keeping cool in the shade.
We stop. Then move on. And the voices fade.
If we're lucky, we will see the rhino.
He makes us smile. And of course, we both know
That she is here with us, part of this Earth.
One cannot measure what this day is worth.
This is us. This is real. We stop and cry
And smile through tears as we inhale the sky.

2016

Romney Marsh

All is still.
I cannot move, engulfed by this awe
Which keeps my boots anchored in the damp grass.
The yellow sun bleeds across the sky
Like a broken egg yolk.
The rays, yet bright and weakly warm,
Bring water to my eyes as I scan the horizon.
I taste the salt in the air as it dries my lips.
A wind-crippled tree hunches over,
Its back speckled with splashes of bright lichen.
The tree, condemned never to change direction.
Beyond, Romney sheep stand dotted about the lush pasture,
Like puffs of steam streaked with coal.
Their lambs gently bleat for reassurance.
I watch as the first curls of mist begin to roll in from the sea,
And I can hear the ghostly whistles of past steam trains.
Underneath my feet, I can feel the faint pulse
Of dead hamlets and lives forgotten.
But there, some way off, historical testimony

In the remains of Hope All Saints Church.
All erect, like members of a ghostly congregation.
Still standing. Still Hope.
A solitary bird wheels overhead.
So, for a moment, I feel less alone.
The yellow fingers of the sun grow thinner
And a darkness grows over my vista.
I make my way home through the dusk
And, as I push through the here and now,
The past falls around my shoulders
Like a comfortable blanket
As, one by one, the stars show themselves
And light my way home.

2017

Old Man, Old Woman

Look at you, old man,
You age and fester now.
Yet, look at me,
Devoid of heart to make you pay
For your selfish game, when
You screwed up my childhood
And threw it away.

Puny, haggard man
Who slowly kills himself.
Avoid you not my eyes
But look me in my face!
Can you really feel shame?
And are you aware that
You debase the human race?

Black cavernous eyes
That transport me in time.
No, Dad! No Dad!
Leave me be! Hurt me no more! Desist!
A second's nightmare – vanished.
Dead eyes cast a look that
Now I can resist.

Then you, old woman,
How your memory wanes
As you talk of
Old times, you butcher's accomplice
Who hacked at my years, left me
Deformed, loveless and cold!
How much did I miss?

Mum, hide me! Please, Mum!
Why do you laugh? He's here!
Please, God, help me!
The pain! Make him stop! Let me run!
Dead eyes cast a look and I –
I can resist. Have you
No faith in your son?

Look at me, old man,
Old woman, look at me.
Can you feel it?
Can you feel what you did? Deceived –
A thousand faces. They left.
They smiled ignorant smiles
And you looked relieved.

Old man, old woman,
Can you know what you lost?
No love. No joy.
I feel what you could never feel.
My heart, protected by her
So sweet, and my own son
Gives succour to heal.

Look again, my eyes.
Nothing to fear. Dead eyes
Within dead souls.
Hearts that lost all without trying.
Time's passed, old man, old woman.
My tears are cold now and
Dead eyes are crying.

1997

Woman's House

Hot, red blood flowing through long veins.
Flowing like water through plastic pipes, gushing and rushing
To fill the bath, soaking in blood sodden brain
Within cold, hard walls: white-washed so stains can be
scrubbed clean.
Primrose white paint in neat kitchen where acids churn and
gurgle
To sanitise mess; bleached and disinfected, wiping away
non-niceties.
Down pipes and pipes that go up, nailed to walls.
Cold, then hot water and blood and non-niceties, flushed
underground.
Close doors then sleep. Open windows then wake.
Enter living room: dark and veined. Pull, push. Pulling.
Pushing.
Pumping life down cables,
Electrified signals send life into joints, hinges, handles, but-
tons, tendons.
Hard, marble sinews; soft, lush layers take the work and strain
As life runs, walks, creeps and flows about shiny, dead follicles.
Neat, straight and corrugated.
Long, dark hallway,
Frightening,
Inviting.
If I ask you in, you'll come.

1997

The Fire

The poor mother rocks her crying child
As she sits by the dying embers of the fire.
'Whisht, whisht,' she whispers
As she wraps her ragged skirt over his bare legs.
Her helplessness makes her feel half wild.

Her two small boys huddle by her feet
And Kathy, wide-eyed, watches the door anxiously.
Her little heart thumps.
'Mammy,' she says, 'I'll go up the road and fetch him.'
She knows she must, if they are to eat.

The girl steps out into the sharp sleet.
Her thin shoes slip around in the horse-dirty mud.
When she nears the pub,
Her mouth grows dry as she hears the chatter inside.
Her arrival here is bittersweet.

On tip toe, she taps on the window.
The landlord sees her and nods at her father.
He opens the door
And the warmth of the blazing fire within wafts out.
Her father's cheek wears a ruddy glow.

He says not a word to his daughter
But sways as he gently puts two coins in her hand.
The door shuts her out.
Kathy bites her trembling lip as she turns to go.
Sweet Kathy, what has this life taught her?

Her father, working hard on the land
Six days a week and Sundays reserved for the Church,
To pray for his sins.
Her mother, worn out with worry and drudgery
As life ebbs away like shifting sand.

A knowing smile in the village store

Greets Kathy, and she buys what provisions she can
With some peat and coal.
'I'll send up my lad,' says the woman with kindness
And a little extra for the poor.

Kathy's wan face raises a weak smile
As she leaves, clutching what she can carry herself.
She feels the cold now.
Her little dress drags in the slush as she goes home.
Kathy walks on through her common trial.

At home, the girl kisses her Mam's cheek.
She revives the fire, then takes the sleeping baby
And sits on the hearth.
All the children watch as their mother makes a meal.
This will be the best they eat all week.

The father staggers through the doorway
But the exhausted sleeping children do not stir.
He sits down meekly
And his wife serves the boiled bacon and potatoes
As she hums a tune of Galway Bay.

He muses now, as he watches his wife.
Her Irish blue eyes meet his and she smiles at him
Then moves beside him
And kisses his weary head as she holds him close,
Feeling the love they had vowed for life.

2017

Respect

Why does my daughter hate this beret?
Is it the way I wear it to one side?

Is it the colour?

I have several colours you know, including black

And black goes with anything. Doesn't it?

'Take it off, Mum, please don't wear it in the hall!'

'All right, all right, I'll take it off just before I go in. I need to keep my ears warm.'

So I took it off just before we entered the school hall for the Christmas fair

But not before Lisa's mum saw me

And Lisa's mum had a perfect perm framing her perfectly made up face.

My hair had gone all static as I took off my beret

And I had to peer at Lisa's mum through the strands of hair sticking to my face.

I don't think my daughter respects me now.

1988

Jelly

Your sweet love pours over me
Like liquid jelly
I soak it up like a sponge
Then I set

You eat me, spoonful by spoonful
And I am all gone.

2016

Caravan Holidays in Corton

Right then, are we ready?
All packed, boxed up and tucked in?
Remembered your toys, the beach ball, slippers, flippers and racquets?
Got the food, the big frying pan and the coats,
The sweets for the journey and huge box of porridge oats?

You definitely gave the key to our neighbour?
And he knows where the pets' stuff is?
I've checked the car for oil and water. Tank's full.
Have we got the receipt, the money, camera and hats?
The big fluffy towels? No, we can't bring the cats!

Wellies, sandals, sun cream and frost bite ointment,
Shorts, ear muffs, gloves and swimsuits?
In you get. Belt up. Snuggle up in the blanket.
We're five minutes down the road, you can't need the loo!
And why are you wearing only one shoe?

Right, shoe's in with the bag full of marbles.
Everyone's comfy, now let's just get going.
We'll head for 'Toby's Walks' where we can stretch our legs.
No, we're not there yet. We've got two hours to go.
When we reach the coast road, I'll let you know.

Come on, everybody out, breathe in that sea air.
What shall we do first? Golf? Tennis?
Swimming, football, ball in the bucket, nearest the line?
Or shall we walk down to the sea?
It's ages before we can make a cup of tea.

Right, we've got the keys, let's get unpacked.
Find the biscuits, the tea bags and milk.
We'll have a swim before Mum starts dinner,
Then we'll go to the club where Dad can have a beer.
Isn't it great to be back another year?

2016

My Love for You

My love for you is as strong as the
Arms you use to work so hard.
My love for you is as deep as the
Eyes that watch me.
My love for you is as high as the
Hopes you have for us.
My love for you is as soft as the
Hair on your precious head.
My love for you is as hard as the
Nails on your fingers.
My love for you is as constant as the
Beats of your beautiful heart.
My love for you is as warm as the
Sweat on your panting chest.
My love for you is as refreshing as the
Air you breathe on my face.
My love for you is as rich as the
Voice that whispers in my ear.
My love for you is as powerful as the
Words I hear you say.
My love for you is as playful as the
Child that sits on your knee.
My love for you is as serious as the
Line that runs across your forehead.
My love for you is as free as the
Laughter that lights up your face.
My love for you
Is this.

1998

Have a Word with Yourself

What's that you say?
No, that's *not* what I said
That's the crazy cat that lives in your head
Or the monster that hides underneath your bed
That's the ghoul that hangs around after dark
Or the oddball that lurks about in the park
It's the gloomy road to the haunted house
The hairy spider or the squealing mouse
It's the half-eaten frog that the cat dragged in
Or the germ-ridden bluebottle circling the bin
It's your fear of failure or your fear of snakes
Or the fact that the shop had run out of cakes
Could be the dust mites or unwashed sheets
Or you've eaten too many sugar-soaked sweets
Perhaps it's that bloke that annoyed you at work
Or that driver who cut you up with a smirk
Maybe you're worried about the new job
Perhaps it's the burnt gravy left on the hob
It could be the unfulfilled dreams that you have
Or the fact that the toilet roll fell down the lav
It may be you've just had a confidence dip
And your brain kicked your arse and said, 'time to let rip'
Whatever it is that's made you see red
Have a word with yourself and don't climb in *my* head!

2016

Milky Stout and Melancholy

If 'ifs' and 'ands' were pots and pans,
There'd be no need for tinkers.

What if you never came over here
And stayed in the land of leprechauns
And neeps and soda bread?

What if you had arrived
And your Feyther had stayed
And looked after you all?

If 'ifs' and 'ands' were pots and pans,
There'd be no need for tinkers.

What if you never tasted farls
And tatties and onions
And porter cake?

What if death had not come
And your Mam had stayed
And loved you for longer?

If 'ifs' and 'ands' were pots and pans,
There'd be no need for tinkers.

What if you were a colleen again
And you still believed in love
And leprechauns?

What if I told you that I'm from there too
And I believe in leprechauns
And I believe in love?

If 'ifs' and 'ands' were pots and pans,
There'd be no need for tinkers.

I know how to cook soda bread and porter cake,
But you never bothered to find out.

1998

Silent Ambulances

I stand and look and feel and ask
Myself, 'what can it be today?'
And all about me people mask
The fears they have and say,
'It's all right, don't fret.'
Mam signals to me, 'come inside!'
While men call out with soundless words
And children run indoors to hide.
I see that all the birds
Have fled the thin wire.
Silent ambulances scream past.
Instinctively, I hold my ears
And wish for times before the blast.
I never saw Mam's tears
When my Da was here.
Inside, I look out on the scene,
A repeat run of yesteryear.
My eyes are burning hot and keen.
I see his face and fear
That Mam sees it too.
Silent ambulances screaming.
Silent mouths saying the same things.
Silent, weeping hearts still dreaming.
Lone, silent bird that sings
Of hope on the wire.

1997

This Life

Don't you ever want to be a million miles from this life?
I'd get a divorce, if I were life's wife.
It presents me with nothing but heartache and strife,
This life.

Don't you ever feel like telling them what to do with their tat,
False promises, old lies and inane chat?
Say, listen up and learn; you're talking through your hat,
Fat cat.

Don't you ever feel completely at the mercy of this place,
Knowing you don't quite fit in with that face?
But we rally each other along, keeping pace.
Mad race.

Don't you ever feel the temptation to run away and hide,
Like the groom who finds he picked the wrong bride?
Like you aimed for the bulls eye and the dart flew wide.
You tried.

Don't you ever want to run naked with the sun on your chest,
Feeling the breeze as you cast off your vest?
And you swing to and fro from the East to the West.
What jest!

Yes, I often want to be a million miles from this life,
Though love does exist where ill will is rife.
I have seen it and felt it as keen as a knife.
My life.

2016

Holding On

Tripping along in her high heeled shoes,
She walks ahead of me, her head held high.
I know the invitation was just a ruse
Forwarded so I could not refuse
So I'm here, just behind, holding her bags.

Once, it was she who embarrassed me,
Standing, screaming in the middle of the shop,
When her heart craved all that she could see.
Then we'd pay for one thing, to her glee,
And she stood, just behind, holding my hand.

Yesterday, as she skipped into school,
She realised, wide-eyed, that I would not stay.
She smiled and the teacher smiled, so cruel,
While acid tears burned on me, the fool,
As I stood by the door, holding her scarf.

In those days, when she was a child
And she cried because that boy asked her out,
Her instinct knew that she had beguiled.
She felt the call of woman, all wild
And I sat on her bed, holding her tight.

Tomorrow she'll use her woman's art
And she will know when her man's been conquered.
She'll marry him and give him her heart,
Her love piercing his mind like a dart.
I'll smile, holding on to my memories.

1999

This Moment

Once, a lifetime ago, I had what you enjoy.
To live in this moment only,
What sweet bliss.
What calm alternative to this.

If I could, I'd make all your moments this moment
And you could feel what you feel now
All your days.
Free from the hurt of this world's ways.

To you, all things possess beauty, all things bring joy.
You know this truth and you feel it.
It is yours.
Keep it. It will open life's doors.

When I am with you, this moment is all there is.
You make me live in the present.
I am alive,
Like the honey bee in the hive.

Like the fox cub we saw in the garden last night
And the flowers that made you laugh,
And your face.
You let me opt out of the human race.

I hope you keep this moment somewhere in your heart

And some part of you remembers,
This is all.
Don't become trapped behind the wall.

All the time I breathe I will remind you of this
And life shall not tether your heart.
You will fly.
You are the Earth. You are the sky.

Once, a lifetime ago, I had what you enjoy.
Now I watch you live this moment
And I smile.
So glad to share it for a while.

2016

Passion Flower

Violet, paper thin petals.
Paper thin, ten true petals, like tissue, fragile yet strong,
Cut and shaped to perfection.
Gentle hue, changing as it melts into the centre,
Pulling the eye towards the ten sepals.
Spiky, soft filaments encircling the rich centre
Where the stigmas are driven into the five anthers;
The passion of the flower.
Tendrils curling and coiling, snapping at the air,
While the beautiful, plump ovary beckons the bees.
Pure, Holy Nature.
Fruit, the food of love, yellow and orange,
Soft and plump;
The passion flower
Meets the passion of Man.

1976

Christmas Sestina

Why do you wish me a Merry Christmas
And a Happy New Year?
The words that spout from your mouth
Mean no more to me than they do to you.
Do you consider this to be the antidote to the world's evil?
Or do you consider nothing at all?

Is this it then, is this all?
A pair of socks and a scarf for Christmas?
Couldn't I have had a blindfold to shut out the evil
Around me, and glide through the New Year
Oblivious to the suffering of others, just like you?
You might have bought me a gag to put on your mouth.

Walk down the street and lips quiver on every mouth,
Like Tiny Tim, 'Merry Christmas, one and all!'
But Tiny Tim does not exist for me. Or for you.
Worry about your pension money at Christmas,
And whether you will be in hospital for the New Year
Wearing a black eye and stitches, calling card of today's evil.

I did my bit you know, I saw the graphics of evil.
But this surreptitious strain that oozes from the mouth
Of the carol singer who wishes me a Happy New Year
Before throwing stones at my window, because all
My change has gone on the paperboy's Christmas
Box; this strain will be the death of me. Or you.
Mr Politician, sir, what will I get from you?
Another promise of winning the fight against evil,

Gift wrapped in your babble like last Christmas,
Sealed with a kiss from your dry mouth?
I'll put it in the cupboard with all
The rest I have saved, year after year after year.

And what shall I give you this year?
My experience and resilience so that you
May learn from me? How can you learn at all
When you are muffled and blinkered by evil,
So much so that you do not look at the mouth
That wishes you a very Merry Christmas.

Can you really stand by and feel the evil
Crawl through the Happy New Year that leaves your mouth?
Is there any chance at all that we may celebrate a truly Merry
Christmas?

1995

How You Make Me Feel

You're my flumptiousness, my scrumptiousness,
My all round plumptiousness,
My all good things rolled into onetiousness,
My come on, let's have some funtiousness.

My cuddly bear, my slobber chops,
My giant-sized bag of chocolate drops,
My 1985 edition of Top of the Pops,
Believe me, you're the absolute tops.

You're my steaming cup of strong Yorkshire tea,
As vital as the honey bee,
The calming breath on my life's rough sea,
You just make me me.

You're like a bunch of my favourite flowers,
You make me feel like I've got special powers,
You're warm and sweet like April showers,
You give meaning to my hours.

This is how you make me feel.
It's unreal, it's the real deal.
You're like a great big hearty square meal.
You're the sweet orange segment inside the peel.

2014

Labora Cum Amora

Oh, leave me alone with your prods and probes
And your well intentioned scratching and scraping.
Will it never end, this cycle of mending,
This forced concrete surgery, meant for the gaping,
Who prod me and probe me again.

All shapes, all sizes, colours and creeds,
Come daily to judge me, standing and staring.
No genuine thought for me. I, sickening
By your bricks and your mortar, constantly baring
My heart and my soul to your eyes.

When once I was a friend to the Pilgrims,
My role was sincere, my heart pumped and I lived
For those who suffered all the pains, to be waiting
Upon bodies and souls whom they loved. Galling
I find it now to watch your face.

What purpose now but to stand and be made
A tourist attraction, luring and snaring
The right kind of clientele, fit for spending
Your money? To be like you, no love or caring
For those in real need of my peace.

For those of you who love me, I give thanks.
For those who bring belief, kneeling and praying,
I humbly respect you. Hear my plea, my calling.
Let Nature's sweet sun and rain devour me, laying
Her gentle hands around my throat.

Nature's euthanasia is welcome
To me now, as they keep probing and prodding,
Relentlessly scratching, constantly scraping.
I'm sore. And still you go by, smiling and nodding,
Using me in my helplessness.

1998

34

Bullen Lane

Ah, I remember Bullen Lane.
The neat converted oast house
With my round bedroom wall,
And the busy thriving garden
Where the fruit canes stood tall.

The car tyre swing strapped to the oak.
I spent many hours on that,
Absorbing the sweet scents;
Cherry blossom, apple and hops,
My delight was immense.

Across the road, primroses
Grew on the banks of the stream;
They twinkled in the sun.
I had a magical time there.
I would run, run and run.

And laugh and dream and lose myself
In the gorgeous openness.
My love of life grew there.
I honed my imagination
As I breathed in the air.

I would walk along Bullen Lane
On Sundays with my mother.
Scared, I would hold her hand,
As the pitch black countryside sky
Enveloped a strange land.

We went to the pub to buy crisps,
Chocolate and lemonade
Served in the saloon bar.
Then headed home to the coal fire,
By the light of the stars.

I would skip across the orchard
And through the farmyard to school,
Running through the willow
That stood on the edge of the pond.
Back then, I did not know

That this is as pure as it gets,
This wonderful Earth, our home.
In childhood, my playground.
Now, my solace, my own haven,
Where peace of mind is found.

I loved my time in Bullen Lane,
Where sweet childhood and Nature
Became mingled as one.
Now, when life is hard, Bullen Lane
Is my enduring sun.

2017

My Sister's Fingers

And so, my light is waning,
As womankind must surely lose her glow,
Then my sister, the Sun, will take you for herself,
Just as *your* sister makes your man her own:

My sister's fingers forage lightly,
Her nails scraping across the surface of your skin.
She grins at me and threatens to describe your sickening
ripeness
As you indulge yourself in her folds.

My sister's fingers forage gently,
Like daggers, piercing the rotten heart of your desire.
She pities me and aims her dangerous rays into your bad eyes,
As you prepare to drown in her delight.

My sister's fingers forage loudly,
As she crackles, silently, above your roaring sea.
She mocks me, and she meets me on the rocks where we first
met,
As you and her lie empty and fulfilled.

My sister's fingers forage kindly,
As she alights upon my tear stained face.
She lifts my heart and I feel whole again,
As you and her become a fading stain.

My sister's fingers forage softly,
Her cursed whispers entering your mind.
She sees my face and thrusts her message deep into your soul,
As you rub out my image from your life.

My sister's fingers forage warmly,
Her icy palms slapping on your skin.
She feels my hurt and beats you with her passion,
As you begin to climb the steps to hell.

My sister's fingers forage hotly,
Her coldness cutting through your fire.
She knows me, and she hates you when the rose spews out its sap
As you give up your nectar to the bee.

My sister's fingers forage fondly,
Like a mother's breath upon her child.
She understands that now the pain must cease, and I am free
As you and she descend into the pit.

2007

Well Done to the Both of Us

As I sit here in this prison with you,
I consider my hard life before you rescued me.

You gave me something I had not foreseen.
You offered me friendship when all about me was mean.
I suppose they didn't want to be bad,
But the name calling, the insults, made me feel so sad.
Then the anger and the vengeance in me
Shaped the course of events. Well, they simply had to be.

And I say well done to the both of us.
One by one we slaughtered them, with very little fuss.
Oh yes, the leering and jeering stopped,
We had our sport and they all dropped.

Too easy to lure them in, stupid fools,
They thought they were special before they lay in great pools
Of their own blood. One good blow to the head
And we watched them leave the living to marry the dead.
I care not that our fun came to an end,
They can't touch me for I have you, my capital friend.

So I say well done to the both of us,
We squeezed out the life from them, as a spot oozes pus.
Their dark, dirty breath crept under the door,
As we gleefully high-fived, sure that they were no more.

Why don't you smile and rejoice with me, friend?
You don't think of leaving me now it's come to an end?
Look at me man, you know I'm a winner
Like my clever friend Hogg, and his Justified Sinner.
As I sit here now, I grow tired and cold,
I feel I can't see you as my eyes grow old.

Still, I say well done to the both of us.
Friend, where have you gone?

2016

Baby, Dear Baby

Oh baby, dear baby,
You beautiful thing.
We tried to imagine
What our love would bring.
We gave you a name,
We pictured your face,
We picked out your clothes
From the very best place.
But here now, in wonder
We look at you there,
And know there is nothing
On Earth to compare
With your sweetness, your wholeness,
Your wonderful glow.
Oh baby, dear baby
Teach us what you know.

1984

One Year and Rising

Ok, I give up, I haven't a clue,
What is it this time that I've failed to do?
I've fed you, I've changed you, I've hummed you a tune,
Shall I play Des O'Connor or read Mills and Boon?
Perhaps a cartoon on the box, but then, no,
I promised myself that I'd not stoop so low
As to calm you and con you with technology,
I'm a 'back to the roots' Mum, all natural, that's me!
Shall I whistle or gurgle or juggle some toys?
Oh, give me a break darling, stop all that noise.
I've got it! I've sussed it. I know where you're at.
You want me to wear that silly old hat.
The one that I cherished and wore all the time,
Till your sticky hands found it and labelled it 'Mine'.
It smells of stale milk now, it's faded and stained,
A bit like my hands only not quite so grained.
Hang on now, I've noticed that glint in your eye,
The tears have stopped now and I'm sure I know why.
You're sporting with me, you mischievous pup,
You're passing your time away playing me up!

1984

The Lemon Bush

The lemon bush, a fitting life
As you start on your journey as husband and wife.

Green, for pastures new you explore.
Yellow, the flames of love as they roar.
Purple new growth, forgiving and deep.
Sweet smelling flowers to make your heart leap.
The lemon fruit, a bitter-sweet jewel,
A sun-yellow coat round a cupful of fuel.
That feeds and sustains and comforts and warms,
Like love in its touch and its sights and its forms.

The lemon bush, a fitting life
As you start on your journey as husband and wife.

2000

Moving House

Do you remember when we moved house?
We didn't have a cat basket
And I said we could put them in a cardboard box.
You said it wasn't a good idea.

I suppose we were a mile down the road
When we heard them scratching and hissing
And you told me to stop the car
But I said, 'don't panic,' and I kept driving.

That's when it happened, just when I said
Don't panic:
One of them squeezed her head through the top of the box
And the other one weed in the bottom of the box.

You screamed,
I pushed her head back in and she bit me.
You felt the warm wee begin to seep through the cardboard
Onto your lap.

I swerved, cursing the cats.
Your cursed me for not listening to you.
They hissed and spat at each other,
Then we arrived outside our new home.

We sat there and cried then we laughed.
I remember that was the day
When you were the parent and I was the child.

2006

A Tribute

Some would blame you, Lord, for what happened to her.
Three months was not long for the rest of her life.
Her fight, in my memory, not dulled by a blur
But clear, alive and sharp as a knife,
That cuts to my heart.

It was not you. It was Fate, filthy and base,
Who grabbed her with his sickening bony grip,
Then thrust his blackened bulging eyes up to her face
And whispered, with his festering lip,
'Your life will end now.'

Oh Lord, if it were you, it might have been short
And less painful. Her suffering heart, perhaps,
Broken less keenly, as when Fate of her made sport.
No mercy, when tentacles it wraps
Tight round a good soul.

Lord, you must have seen the way this woman fought.
Disgusting Fate came up against a fighter
Who would not give, but live. Each day became a thought,
Sustaining, making dark nights brighter,
Though death hid nearby.

Not enough, stealing what was not his to take,
Fate called upon his old and great companion,
False Hope. Together they conspired to create fake
Signs of healing and strength, until she
Believed she could win.

Their trick discovered, she stumbled on the road,
And we carried her as far as she allowed.
Through courage and determination her fear showed,
But she fought on and never once bowed
To her tormentors.

Then, Lord, you found her and took her in your arms.
Her battered heart found comfort, her troubled mind
Found peace. You wrapped her in your cooling, calming balms;
Fate and False Hope were banished, and kind
Truth enveloped her.

Three months became four, five, six and then a year.
The battle, though bravely fought, she could not win.
Acceptance never was accepted, life was dear.
Her thoughts and reflections kept within,
As she lay dying.

Lord, if dignity and spirit be the key
To life's end, then she unlocked the door to you.
Remember how she died, swallowed by the big sea,
Loved by the insignificant few
Who fought beside her.

1992

Promised Land

What is your intention
As you write out this prescription?
Will it really make me better?
Do I get my Doctor's letter?
For I'm not below the breadline
And I heard it through the grapevine, that
They'll lower it again,
When the Budget is announced.

Pardon me for seeming,
As you hand it to me beaming,
Just a little bit ungrateful
For I find the guesswork hateful.
Is the medicine important?
Then again, perhaps I oughtn't to
Ignore this depression,
So I'll take the tablets please.

No, I can't stay off all week.
The bedroom roof has sprung a leak
And the Missus wants it mending,
On account of Jan's unending
Bouts of asthma. Lord, she suffers,
But the Doctor gave her puffers and
Some medicine to take
Which we give her every night.

Oh yes, we own our own home.
They offered us a great big loan.
So we bought it from the council,
Needing very little counsel,
For we saw a documentary,
And the rest is elementary, and
We want the very best
For our children, ain't that right?

Now this chest infection
Is the fifth since the election.
But I've got my Doctor's letter
And I'm sure that I'll get better,
As soon as I begin the course
Which Maggie says she may endorse
For everyone. She promised
Us a cure for all our ills.

1993

At the Foot of the North Downs

Do you remember our little home at the foot of the North Downs?
Of course, you would not forget.
We loved to go out and walk along the rough track
With the buddleia brushing along our faces and the cool ferns
tickling our legs.
I picked plump blackberries that stained my fingers purple,
And I would feed them to you.
At the end of the track, we reached the reservoir,
Its hard metal fencing out of place in the wilderness that was
the disused quarry.
Tall grass, buttercups, deep green ivy and willowy trees;
We would pick our way through to reach the river
And watch the dragonflies and the water skaters.
We walked along for a bit, arm in arm, then made our way
towards the dusty road,
Where lorries once trundled up and down.
You would walk in front, beating back the brambles and the
nettles for me,
Then over the stile to the edge of the corn field.
Hot yellow corn, tall and upright,
Gently swaying in the sunny breeze.
You knew what I would do because you knew I couldn't resist it;
I pulled off my dress and ran naked ahead of you,
And you watched me, laughing.
I would turn and run back towards your open arms,
Always that thrilling danger of being seen.
You did not want anyone else to see me,
But you knew I had to do it.
We would kiss.
Reluctantly I would put the dress back on
And we would amble back, hand in hand, to our little home
At the foot of the North Downs.

2016

Trees

I like to hug a tree. There, I said it,
And of those who judge me, how many have tried it?
Do you not want to know the history?
Can you not see the wonder and the mystery?
Open your mind and you will hear them speak;
They will give you the reassurance that you seek.
Press your cheek against the bark so tender.
Stay and feel the energy, for it will render
You speechless. Your heart will pound against your chest
As the energy from that tree fills you with zest.
Do they not tell you what they've seen and heard?
All the people, all the skies, every fox and bird.
All the wars, all the changes, all the love,
From way down in the Earth, to magical realms above.
I put my arms right round and hold it tight.
I can feel its beauty and I can feel its might.
I feel connected when I hug a tree.
I give thanks for its spirit, pulsating through me.
Such power has not been endowed by chance;
From the tiniest twig to the most immense branch.
To not notice is simply to be lost.
Trees make you and me. We ignore them at our cost.

2017

Change

There you are love, he's gorgeous
But...........
Darling, he's just like me with your nose
Oh...................
Just give me your arm, we need some blood
Why?..............
That's it, let him suckle, he can do it
How?...................
Let's get you cleaned up and onto the ward
What about?...............
Clever girl, you managed it all on your own, didn't you?
Did I?...............
You're a Mum!
Yes......................

1985

You Weren't Always This Big

I could hold you in one hand once upon a time.
You in the expensive shirt and the designer shades,
You weren't always this big.
I could bring a smile to your face just by poking out my
tongue,
And you did not feel seriousness.
I could make you warm and comfortable, in a snug cot,
After a long and filling sup on your mother's milk.
That was all you needed.
You in the jeans and the only trainers to be seen in,
You with the silly girlfriend hanging on your voice,
You with the mobile phone and the state of the art laptop.
You weren't always this big.
And I wasn't always this small.

1999

Baby

You lay there, a wondrous example of the human form.
My eyes, drunk in your presence, sting with emotion.
My heart is afloat on a beautiful ocean
Of love and awe and fear.

I stand there, a humbled receiver of a parent's gift.
My mind, heightened at your sight, is all devotion,
And your eyes drown me, secure in the notion
That I will carry you.

1984

Limerick

There was a young girl who worked very hard,
She fancied herself as a latter-day Bard,
So she wrote every day,
And created a play,
Which was judged to be too avant-garde.

2017

Funny

Wouldn't it be fun
Ny if we all communi
Cated in Haikus?

1998

What You Mean to Me

I love you to the moon and back a million times and some more.
There are not enough minutes from here to the end of time
For me to explain what you mean to me.
You are a miracle.
I gave you life but you gave me more.
Because of you, my life has meaning.
Because of you, I notice the flowers,
I feel this Earth. We are part of this Earth.
I have watched you grow in every sense.
You taught me to be patient.
You taught me not to be scared of the world.
You are my miracle.
My love is too vast, too frightening,
Too wild to contain in mere syllables.
I just feel it.
And I hope you feel it too.
These lines are but grains of sand
On the vast shores of language and imagination;
These words are but drops
In the ocean of all that is mankind's existence.
You help me to see the world through your eyes.
You are Grace and Significance,
You are Courage and Love,
You let me be a child again.
I love you to the moon and back a million times and some more.

2014

That Smile

That smile is all I'll ever need.
My heart will follow that smile's lead.
That smile will get you anywhere,
Anything and everywhere.

That smile is like a piece of cake,
Hot chocolate and cool milkshake.
That smile is like a perfect rose,
It warms my fingers and my toes.

That smile can make me laugh or cry,
It's my hard rock, my lullaby.
That smile can dance within my soul,
It breaks me up and makes me whole.

That smile can carry me away,
It lights my night and makes my day.
That smile is naughty, sweet and true,
It's all I want, because it's you.

That smile is all I'll ever need,
My heart will follow that smile's lead.
That smile will get you anywhere,
Anything and everywhere.

2016

Night Watch

I stood and watched the moon last night,
She lit up the sky.
The beautiful, beautiful clouds were floating by;
Silver white hems on black, deep blue,
Then pink tinged and grey.
They shade her kind face before drifting away.
She smiled down on me, the good moon
And the clouds thinned out.
Then I saw how the Autumn wrought leaves lay about.
The half clothed trees whispered to me,
Ghostly silhouettes.
They shivered as the night spiders cast out their nets.
Her rays twinkled through the branches,
Landing at my feet.
I could feel her coolness and I could feel her heat.

I stood and watched the moon last night,
She lit up the sky.
I was bathed in her awe and I wanted to cry.
The grass, laced with silver ribbons,
Dense with the creatures
That toil through the night, without showing their features.
The moon's spotlight falls on a tail
And the mouse is shy.
A whisker, a grey coat or the gleam of an eye.
The silent fox stops and walks on.
The flap of a wing,
Then note by beautiful note, the birds start to sing.
She is a miracle, this moon,
And she comforts me.
Her wonderful presence reminds me to just be.

2016

What Can I Do?

What can I do? What can I do?
When the worst thing in the world has happened to you.
My heart is breaking, breaking, aching for you,
And for her.

What can I say? How can I mend?
When the life that you cherished has come to an end.
Let me hold you, my child. Let me hold you close,
Close to her.

Where are we now? What have we left?
When this black cloud engulfs us and leaves us bereft?
We must hold on, my child, hold on tight,
Hold on to her.

Can I show you? Is it in me?
Have I got the strength to make you see
That we still have love, we still have faith,
We still have her.

2016

You

You're my trip to the moon
My egg and my spoon
My stars in the sky
My reason why
You're the Bee Gees hits all rolled into one
You're the soft summer breeze, the warmth of the sun
You're the reason I can
You're my number one fan
The perfect snowflake
The chances I take
You're the answer to my question
My cure for indigestion
My reason for being
My hearing and my seeing
You're my favourite sweets
All kisses and treats
You're my penny from heaven
My lucky number seven
My day at the zoo
You're just................you.

2016

Sports Day

I look at her with a confident grin,
Careful not to betray
The trembling state of my nerves within,
On this momentous day.
She smiles at me with that beautiful smile,
We make a secret pact.
Our hearts reach out and entwine for a while,
I'm ready to react.
The crowd is hushed at the shrill whistle sound,
My heart is beating fast.
Arms flail, teeth grit and desperate feet pound,
No one wants to be last.
I fear to look lest I see a folly,
A grin plays on her face.
She watches as I receive my lolly,
I won the Mummy race!

1987

Not for Sale

You think you can buy me?
You think you can buy my chest? My heart?
You think you can buy my head?
My eyes, my ears, my tongue?
Look at me
I am me
I am a breathing, thinking, living me
You think you can own me?
You think you can own my fingers, my toes?
You think you can own my feet, my knees?
My back, my buttocks, my groin?
Just look at me
I am me
I am not yours
I am not anyone's
You cannot buy me on your credit card
You have no mortgage on me
You took out no loan on me
You did not purchase me on one of your store cards
You cannot collect loyalty card points on me
I am not for sale
I am mine, not yours
You cannot own me
You would know that if you knew what love is.

2017

My Cloak

I wear my cloak every day.
It fits me perfectly,
Made to measure.

Some days it feels as light as summer rain,
Other days it feels so heavy,
As if it is sodden with the tears of all the world.
Then I find it almost too much to bear,
My shoulders stoop with the weight,
And the chill eats into my bones.

On better days, it flaps gently about me
So that, no matter what I do, I am always aware of it being there.
But on those better days, my cloak moves with me.
It must do, as it is a part of me,
Just like my arm or my leg or my heart.

On the difficult, heavy days,
My cloak is like a dark growth that has attached itself to my body
And it presses down on me.
I must endure its forever presence,
For it is with me until the end,
Until that day when I can unclasp it from around my neck
And let it fall to the Earth.

On that happy day, I will leave my cloak behind.

2016

Another Springtime

So another springtime has arrived
And I don't remember the summer before,
Though the faded glow of the hot sun's kiss
Still lives on my skin.
I can see the pulp of the unswept leaves
That lies in the shadows
Of unpruned trees and bushes
That stood in the autumn rain.
And what of the winter?
I have no recollection, save the cold,
As his frosty, ice-laced breath, chilled my bones,
And it was so, so dark.

So another springtime has arrived.
I can see the yellow jewels on the japonica,
Popping out like spangles.
The snowdrops have already beaten the rush,
As the daffodils and tulips, the crocus and the hyacinth
Still use their energy to push through the earth.
And the flowering cherry tree.
The flowering cherry tree is fit to burst its buds
In a display of pink tremendousness.
My raw grief moves over now,
Making way for numb sadness
And I had not noticed
How dull my eyes had become.
But now the springtime snatches up my senses
And I can anticipate with joy,
The pink blossom on the tree.

2017

It Wouldn't Be the Same Without You

Pushing and weaving our way through the hordes, nervously wearing a smile,
Train drivers, monsters and pirates with swords, distracting me for a while,
Then whoosh! And zoom! And screams growing loud.
Contorted faces rush from the crowd.

And then I remember what my job is, and why I find myself here.
There's no need to get myself in a tizz, no reason for me to fear.
I'm just here to take care of the coats, take piccies, read maps and make some notes.

It's not that I'm frightened, I'm really not. I just volunteered, you see.
You must understand that someone's got to queue for eats and tea,
And plan the shortest route to the loo, and stand by, ready to cheer or boo.

'But what of the summer,' I hear you cry, 'when you don't need all this stuff?
When the sun beams down and you're warm and dry and you travel light enough?
Surely then you can join in the fun, brave the Ghost Train or ride the Snake Run?'

Ah, but it isn't as simple as that. The sun brings complications.
What with parasols, sun cream and sun hats. And where's the
First Aid station?
Then there's the need for drinks and ice creams. Someone
needs to be head of the team.

It's not that I'm frightened, I'm really not. I just volunteered,
you see.
You must understand that someone's got to step forward,
and that's me.
They can scream on the trains, planes and boats.

I'm happy just holding the coats.

2013

Shopmania

Now, where shall I start, there's so much I need;
Some boots, some books and a bottle of mead.
Look over there, there's a ten-gallon hat,
There'll come a time when I might need that.
Whoops, 'scuse me love, I'll have those,
I need some super support panty hose.
I must have a long-handled torch for the fog
And look at that wonderful coat for the dog
We might get one day.

I think you'll find I saw that first,
If you put it on you'll be fit to burst.
Besides, I've been after a green waistcoat
That's made from the skin of a mountain goat,
And pictures of fishes,
And three gold rimmed dishes.
I want that film, with the actor I like,
And I simply can't live without a new bike
For the exercise regime I'll start some time.

Now, you get the teapot. I know we've got two
But we don't have one in purple and blue.
I'll get the mop head and pick up a pen.
Then we'll go to the farm shop and choose a nice hen
For the small holding we're planning when we retire.
Someone just said the beef is half price,
And a couple of cacti would be quite nice.
Now is that the lot? We've been here for hours,
What did we come in for? Oh I know, some scourers.

2016

66

Friends

Friends, they come and go.
Some for life, some for show,
Others drift by in a transient glow.
Some I trust with my feelings and thoughts,
Others are those with whom I've argued and fought.
Some, where loyalty scores a big nought.
Some play sincere with a skilful knack,
Then they talk about me behind my back;
They hate in me the things they lack.
Unfortunately it took me a while
To recognise the serpent's smile
On the faces of those who nurse their bile.
Thankfully, the truth will out
And the most false ones are the ones who shout
As they shake my hand, while stifling a pout.
I don't need those, they mean me harm.
Real friends are the ones that bring me calm;
They wash over me like a soothing balm.
I've been fooled. I've been used.
No doubt they were all highly amused.
My conscience is clear, I'm not the accused.
I simply found my trust misplaced,
And wish that I had not embraced
Where honesty had never graced.
But experience is never without worth.
And something we all come to learn from birth
Is that good and bad exist upon this Earth.

Friends, they come and go,
And all of us must surely know,
That what we reap is what we sow.

2016

Moon

We're looking at her now
Our faces reflected in a sun-kissed mirror
Together, your hand in mine in the darkness below her
I cannot be separate from you
And I cannot be separate from her
She ties me to you as she anchors me to this Earth
Remember this time
For when we are not watching her together
When one of us stands here alone
I shall still be looking at her and so will you
From somewhere
And we shall each be smiling at the other in that sun-kissed
mirror.

2010

Teacher

I've sailed the sea of stormy water
I did what I did
And didn't what I oughta
Through thick and thin I made my way
Through lots of pain for little pay
And as I move to pastures new
I take a lasting thought of you
My colleagues who supported me
You bought me cakes and made me tea
You smiled and gave me sound advice
You always seemed so very nice
Until the day I realised
You fed me on a pack of lies
You told me that this job was great
And here I am in such a state
My nerves are bad, I never sleep
A gibbering wreck, I want to weep
There's nothing left, farewell, goodbye
Unless, of course, you need supply.................

1998

Tinnitus

Thirstily drinking in my silence and my peace of mind,
Insidiously running through me, jumping from nerve to nerve,
Laughing at my desperate attempts
To hold on to my composure
And my vigour and my sense of humour.
Intent on spoiling my interaction
With people, with music, with the Earth.
Grinning its demonic grin as I strain
To hear the birds above the scream
And cackling when I must tear myself away from my refuge,
the sea.
Never giving me a moment's respite, save when exhaustion
brings sleep.
Numbing my ability to enjoy the creativity brought about by
cogitation,
Iniquitous in its intention, as it wraps itself around my head,
Tapping into my sanity, sucking it out drip by drip,
Unwavering, unimaginable, unending.

2016

Ants

Four fifteen in the morning
Tick tick tick
And counting
Four sixteen in the morning
Tick tick tick
And on and on and on
They're stirring, burning, on the move
Tramp tramp tramp
Ants walking through my brain
Messing with my mind again
They'll make me go insane
Like the son of Shakespeare's Dane
They're giving me this pain
Drowning me in blood red rain
Will they never refrain?
Clogging artery and vein
My bursting brain brain brain
Lucidity on the wane
Visualize the lane!
Just visualize the lane
Feel the sun, smell the rain
Remember I am urbane
I can't see round the chicane!
Is it still there? The lane?
Persecution
Inhumane

Ants walking through my brain
Messing with my mind again

Five twenty one in the morning

Tick tick tick

And counting

Five twenty two in the morning

Tick tick tick

Tick tick tick tick tick tick tick .... tick.

2016

*The following six poems are
especially for my granddaughter Niamh
who passed away at the age of ten and a half months*

Hello Sweetheart

Hello sweetheart, welcome to our world
You look wonderful, all purple and pink
You're a page in our book, the imperative link
You're early, sweetheart; no matter, you're fine
You're the best accolade to the family line
And we watch you, your fingers all curled

Our hearts ache with love for you, sweetheart
Your little knees bent and your arms tucked in
It's a wondrous sensation to have you as kin
Your tiny lips twitch as you calmly sleep
Your soft eyelids flicker as you steal a short peep
And your knowing gaze hits like a dart

Can you hear us sweetheart, as we talk?
You're growing bigger and bigger each day
We can see that you're stronger in every way
You hold Granddad's thumb and wrinkle your nose
You shout for your tea and you can twiddle your toes
In the blink of an eye you will walk

Oh cuddles are wonderful, sweetheart
And now that you're home we have lots and lots
You've successfully tied up our heartstrings in knots
We watch as you grow, you sit and smile
You'll be laughing and chatting in but a short while
Sweetheart, nothing can rend us apart.

2014

322 Days

She breathed on this Earth for 322 days
What would you do with 322 days?
Sail around the world
Write a book
Take up a course in woodwork
Learn to speak French
Waste them on booze
Renovate a house
Plan a wedding
Nothing much
Walk around Great Britain's coastline
Grow a beard
Waste them on pills
Attend counselling sessions
Train for a marathon
Plan a garden for the Chelsea flower show
Get to know someone better
Do up an old Morris Minor
Throw them away on a smoking habit
Learn to swim really well
Or would you simply love someone?

2015

Goodbye Sweetheart

Goodbye sweetheart. That's so hard to say
Your sweet presence changed our lives forever
Life was wonderful when we were all together
The joy you gave can never be measured
The memories will be eternally treasured
Now we're left and you're taken away

My heart aches to hold you, my sweetheart
One more of our smiley cuddles, that's all
And I look at your photograph there on the wall
What fun when we saw you on Saturday
How could we guess you'd be leaving us Thursday?
Darling, hearts such as ours do not part

I find this serenity horrid
All pretty in pink with your arms tucked in
The blanket wrapped tight and tucked under your chin
One last kiss, sweetheart, one last painful touch
In what way can I bear this? The pain is too much
The long road ahead will be torrid

Sweetheart, we were lucky to have you
You nurtured us, taught us and loved us so
Who can blame us for not wanting to let you go?
But we do, sweetheart, with love and a smile
For we know we will see you in but a short while
When our passage to heaven is due.

2015

Things I Had Not Planned To Do

I went to visit you a thousand times
You and your twin brother
For cuddles and chats and laughs
I had not planned to visit you at the undertakers

I prayed for you every single day
That you would be strong and healthy
That you would continue to grow and thrive
I never dreamt I would be praying for you in Heaven

I bought you toys and clothes and teethers
I showed you lights and pretty things
This Christmas I bought a beautiful glass bauble
And put it on the Christmas tree by the brightest star
In memory of you

I walked around the garden with you
So many wonders to behold
We two especially enjoyed the blossom on the pear tree
What sweet horror that now I should plant primroses on your
grave

I smiled a million smiles with you
We talked and sang and played
I cried tears of joy over you
Now I just cry.

2015

The Roar of The Sea

This is my home,
Here.
Where the roar of the sea
Beats back the roar in my head.
The old, old pebbles rolling underneath my feet.
Here, I am reminded of my mortality
And I like it.
I recall the words I read out at your funeral.
The image of the little boat disappearing over the horizon,
And I can see it now.
I want to wade into the crashing waves
And walk on, following you.
I see myself on the other side of that magical horizon,
And you are there, calling me and smiling.
Yes, the roar of the sea beats back the roar in my head,
But oh, how it beckons my heart.

2015

A Rainbow from Heaven

What's it like to see a rainbow from Heaven, darling?
From here, I usually notice too late,
As the bow is beginning to fade in the sky.
I never see the beginning or the end.

For you, sweetheart, it must be wonderful
To see the raindrops work their magic in the sunlight.
To watch the glorious colours spread
And see one end all the way to the other.

There isn't really a pot of gold, is there my darling?
That was just a story my mother told me and I told you;
Who wants gold?
You gave me something of more value than all gold,
all materials on this Earth.

You, my darling, are my rainbow,
You are my beginning and my end,
You are my raindrops and my sunlight,
And one day we'll watch rainbows together from Heaven.

2015

The Sky and All It Holds

Bright azure blue from here to eternity,
Streaks of creamy sugar cane clouds,
And big cotton puffed up pillows.
Raindrops, warm and soft on your skin.
Raindrops, cold and hard on your head,
The sort that take away your breath and make you laugh.
Early morning sun creeping through the life giving leaves,
Peeping over the hoary hedges and settling on your face.
Hot midday sun, high as forever,
Bathing you in peace and calm and relaxation.
Birds that soar, birds that hover,
Birds that flit and dive and glide.
They tweet and squawk and sing and call,
Their voices pushing through the thick air.
Angry black thunder clouds and blinding light,
Sweet fresh air and hot heavy air.
Lazy bees droning overhead, before soaring up and up.
Gentle butterflies, each wing a work of almost transparent art.
Cold frosty streams of breath in an icy air,
Petal soft snowflakes falling from dense, swollen clouds.
Bats wheel and squeal in an inky pool of light
And the grey clouds rush past a pale moon;
The huge, kind, bright moon that illuminates this Earth.
Insects hum and chop their way through the heavy summer haze.
Every second of every day presents us with a different sky,
A new wonder, a new sight, a new sensation.
Another reason to celebrate life;
The sky and all it holds,
This is my gift to you.

2016

A Poem That I Wrote

My friends, I beg you listen to a poem that I wrote,
It's shorter than a novel though longer than a note.

I agonised for days and weeks, drowned in a flow of troughs and peaks.

What shall I give them? What shall I bring?

The subject matter, that was the thing!

I thought of cats and dogs and mice, of sausages and beans and rice.

Or what about the sun? The moon? A dish that ran off with a spoon?

It wouldn't do, I couldn't see! What shall I write? Oh, woe was me!

I wondered o'er vales and hills,

I almost took to drink and pills,

When all at once, I saw a crowd, a host of golden daffodils!

That cheered me up, the clouds were gone. I knew that I could carry on.

The pressure grew, I writ and writ,

But it sounded like a load of..................rubbish!

I'll never be a Shelley, a Byron or a Keats,

I faced the truth then comfort ate on chocolate and sweets.

I suffered for my art and the sugar gave me grief.

To reach the end of such a task was wonderful relief.

My friends, now that you've listened to the poem that I wrote,

I hope you feel my agony before you cast your vote.

It isn't up there with the good and great of poetry,

But writ with love and flumptiousness, a gift to you from me.

2012

Notes to Poems

A Walk with Charles Dickens

That Charles Dickens is loved and talked about and celebrated all around the world and that his stories are interpreted again and again through different media, is testimony to his genius and his popularity. It is well documented that Dickens lived in Medway as a child and moved back as an adult where he eventually died at Gad's Hill Place. I live in Rochester, a town worth visiting at any time, but particularly during the Dickens Festivals held in June and December. At these times, one can imagine being there in Victorian Britain, sharing the pavement with Mr Charles Dickens. It was this thought that inspired my poem.

The Royal Military Canal

The coastal town of Hythe in Kent is my favourite place away from home. The Royal Military Canal stretches 28 miles from Seabrook near Hythe to Cliff End in East Sussex. Part of the canal at Hythe runs alongside the local zoo. My husband and I like to cycle this route and I'm always excited to know that I may see a giraffe or a rhinoceros on one side of me, while on the other I can see swans and ducks and squirrels. We sought comfort here after our granddaughter passed away. This is a very special place to me.

Romney Marsh

Romney Marsh in Kent is the most magical and sublime area of natural interest and historical significance. It offers villages and seaside towns, vast swathes of open countryside and hidden ruins from past life. Every time I go back, I discover something new. It inspires my life and my work.

Old Man, Old Woman

I once read an account given by a man in his fifties, who had been bullied and beaten by sadistic parents. He was clearly still deeply affected by his experience and so brave to talk about it. I was struck by the frightening power in the hands of parents and the potential for bad or inadequate parents to wreak havoc in a child's life. I like to think we live in a society where people are less likely to ignore something that causes concern. Thankfully, there are many more good people on this Earth than there are bad.

Woman's House

I wrote this when my life was especially hectic. I kept home for my husband and three children, a dog and two cats. I was driving up and down the motorway to Canterbury several times a week where I was studying for a degree in English and Education. Often my children came along with me, sitting in on lectures or doing their homework in the library. Sometimes it felt as though my mental, physical and emotional states all merged into a mad mix and I might spontaneously combust; I didn't.

The Fire

My inspiration for this poem was the tales I heard in my family about Irish fathers going to the pub with their wages and children being sent out to tap on the windows to ask for a few pounds to take home to Mam. Hardworking worn out men who did not easily show the more tender emotions and tired women doing what they could with what little they had. My late grandmother had a hard life. She was a strong woman who moved her children from Northern Ireland to Kent. She was a wonderful Nan to me.

Respect

Who hasn't experienced hat hair just at the wrong moment? I have a lot of electricity in my body; I often receive shocks when I come into contact with escalators, door handles, car doors, vacuum cleaners and more. My daughter is the same. We once went to kiss each other and a spark flashed between our noses. Much screaming and laughing followed. So incidences such as the one described in this poem are not entirely my fault.

Jelly

Sharing love is all that matters. Love takes on infinite forms and delivers on many levels. It could be the smile I exchange with someone I pass in the street, or the pleasantries spoken between myself and the person who serves me in the shop. It could be when I hold open the door for someone who is struggling, or when I listen to a work colleague who is having a bad day. It's the way I feel when my husband looks at me, when my grandchild's little hand reaches for mine, the big hug I share with my child, or the cat purring on my lap. The list is endless.

Caravan Holidays in Corton

Most years as our children grew up, we would take a holiday on a caravan site in the village of Corton between Lowestoft and Great Yarmouth. It is still there on the cliff top with the North Sea rolling in and the Easterly wind blowing. Toby's Walks was the toilet stop off at Blythburgh. Some years we would return home golden brown, sand blasted by the wind and kissed by the sun. Other times we would be frozen and our t-shirts and shorts remained unpacked. Not knowing what was in store and how the weather could change was always part of the fun. We were prepared for anything and our holidays were action packed. They were the best of times.

My Love for You

A poem for my husband. We have been together a long time. We started out with nothing, living in a semi-converted farm building a kindly man let us inhabit on the understanding Frank would do what he could to tidy up the place. One task, I remember, was to screed the kitchen floor ,which had a gulley running across it, leading outside through a hole in the wall. That was where they used to wash the sheep. We've come a long way and experienced some tough times. Our biggest achievement is our family. We still hold hands and we still make each other laugh.

Have a Word with Yourself

Over the course of my life, I have come across a few dissatisfied people. We've all met at least one. They start picking on others, complaining, bickering, bringing attention to themselves. And others are left asking, 'what did I do?' or 'what was that all about?' Jealous people, resentful people, people just having a hard day, who want to spoil the world for others and bring them down. Or maybe someone is simply in a bad mood. Whatever.

Milky Stout and Melancholy

The refrain in this poem is something my grandmother used to say to me when I dithered or protested. She told me about the Irish tinkers who travelled from town to town selling and repairing pots and pans and sharpening knives.

Silent Ambulances

In the 1970s I was affected by the news reports concerning IRA bombings. I had grown up with stories from my Irish family describing how children were taught to hate and throw stones at each other. I remember being in a store in Maidstone when everyone had to leave because of a bomb threat. It turned out to be a hoax and it frightened me very much. I tried to imagine living with

that fear every day. Parents worried for their children. Children
losing parents. People affected mentally, physically, emotionally.
There is hope. History shows war and hatred can stop if people
want it to.

This Life

I am not a pessimist but hear me out. I believe the world is slowly
going mad. There are people starving while others walk into a
supermarket and choose from sixty different loaves of bread and
thirty different kinds of jam. Some people have only short lives
and would give anything to be able to grow older, while others
are having their skin hacked about because they don't want to
get older. Our environment is full of pointless unnecessary tat, on
which we spend millions in trying to dispose of it. And I think my
friend Carolyn and I may be the only ones left on the planet who
write proper letters to each other, using pen and paper.

Holding On

This poem is for girls everywhere and for the mums who love them.
I remember those days when I knew I was changing. Boys fancied
me and I fancied David Soul from Starsky and Hutch. One day
you want to be a child and you need Mum's hugs and advice.
Another day you consider yourself grown up and you simply want
her to leave you alone. As a mum, it isn't always easy to gauge
which day is which. Ultimately, one has to do what a mum does
best. Just be there.

This Moment

When I watch my grandchildren I am reminded of what I had
as a child and how I lost it without noticing. That is the ability
to live in the now without looking back or trying to see what's
in front. Children do this naturally. Every moment holds some
wonder; a new sight, a new sound, a new word, a new game,
something scary, something fun. They just experience it and move

on to the next moment. So I try hard now, to live in the moment. This is the best lesson I can teach my children and their children.

Passion Flower

I was inspired to write this poem when I came across the allegory connecting the passion flower to the story of Jesus Christ. We had the most beautiful passion flowers each year in our garden at the foot of the North Downs. Whether or not one believes that the ten petals represent the ten faithful apostles of Jesus, or that the five stamens represent the five wounds inflicted upon Him, is irrelevant. The sheer perfection and the staggering beauty of the bloom and the plant as a whole is breathtaking and that is enough.

Christmas Sestina

I wrote this after a particularly upsetting news story appeared on the television. An elderly gentleman had been mugged, his wallet and shopping stolen. I don't know much about politics and I don't bother to learn. I do, however, believe that unless mentally incapacitated, every one of us knows right from wrong and when a person chooses to do wrong, he or she must be justly punished. It is always heartening when people rally round and help, especially today when social media is used for the good. We're not a bad lot, really but we have a few miscreants among us.

How You Make Me Feel

These words were inspired by all the people in my life who make me feel good. You know who you are. The slobbery kissers, the big huggers, the listeners, the advisors, the tea and sympathisers. You are all simply there for me. I believe in a Universal truth; love is what counts and without it the world would be a worthless barren nonentity. You all give me love and confidence and energy. I hope you know I'm here for you too.

Labora Cum Amora

When I wrote this, I particularly had in mind Canterbury Cathedral, after watching a group of tourists file past taking photographs, pointing and chattering. I was also influenced by Geoffrey Chaucer's 'Canterbury Tales.' I know we have a responsibility to protect these buildings and I know we need money to do so, hence the visitors and the tea shops and the souvenirs. We do what we do for the right reasons, but I wanted to imagine the situation from the perspective of the tired old structure.

Bullen Lane

Bullen Lane is in the village of East Peckham in Kent. It hasn't changed much since I was a child. I spent a lot of time playing on my own and one of my favourite pastimes was to swing on the old tyre my Dad had rigged up on a huge tree in the garden. I would sing and kick out my toes like the beautiful ladies in the films we watched on television. I roamed around on the farm where my parents worked and looked forward to the summer when my Nan and my cousin would come to stay.

My Sister's Fingers

I was in the process of writing this poem when I read a newspaper article concerning a woman who had carried out an affair with her sister's husband. I felt horrified by the idea of that level of betrayal. The poem had started out as a battle of power between the Moon and the Sun. It became an allegory for base human behaviour and destructive relationships.

Well Done to the Both of Us

I was inspired to write this after reading James Hogg's 'The Private Memoirs and Confessions of a Justified Sinner', around the time the murders of several young men were reported in the news. I like to read about or meet people who may be considered to be eccentric and I am fascinated by the idea that the line between genius and madness is a fine one. The mind is a marvellous and fascinating entity with immense power. It is my belief that we have barely begun to understand its complexities; I find that both thrilling and frightening.

Baby, Dear Baby

I was a very young mum. Some people equate age and life experience with being a good parent, yet we may witness and certainly read about many examples that make nonsense of this notion. The ability to be a loving and engaged parent comes from within. Some people are too immature and self centred to wholly connect with their children. Neither are money and materials the measure of engaged parents. It is all about love and the ability to truly feel it. Love is not something that can be faked.

One Year and Rising

The madness, the fun, the tiredness, the frustration, the worry, the joy, the pride, the chaos, the demands and on and on. We were very happy in our old farm house in Boxley Village with three children under the age of five years, Toby the dog, two cats and a huge grey rabbit my husband had rescued from a building site. It is great fun now to be playing and being silly with our grandchildren like we did back then with our children. To let go of the child within me would be unimaginable.

The Lemon Bush

I was inspired to write about the lemon bush after I saw one in a garden centre. I was amazed it grew in our cooler climate and it was beautiful. The analogy of the journey embarked upon by a newly married couple grew around the plant.

Moving House

I remember this day well. As ever, money was tight and I thought I would save some by putting our cats in a cardboard box rather than buying a made for purpose cat box. My daughter warned me against it and I didn't listen. Tessa pushed her head through the top with an angry look, her ears flattened down for battle. Sooty, the more timid one, did what any anxious cat would do. That day, I learned not to disregard the advice of my child and not to underestimate the power of an angry cat.

A Tribute

I was inspired to write this poem by my dear late Aunt, who was diagnosed with cancer of the brain. Her stoicism was both humbling and heartbreaking. She was a no nonsense person who kept herself well informed. She knew that, after dealing with cancer some years before, there was the possibility it would return. I would keep her company and drive her out and about. Along with other family members and friends, we talked and laughed, played board games and watched television together. I would like to have known her longer.

Promised Land

I recall the financial crash of 1987 when our next door neighbours lost their home. We struggled and they were frightening times. A lot of people had purchased their houses from their local council; the late Prime Minister, Margaret Thatcher, had advocated the idea that everyone was entitled to own their own home. What struck me at the time, was the meanness of the banks and building societies. People who had never missed a mortgage payment were given no sympathy and no help. All people needed was a little more time to recover. Hardworking honest people who were brushed aside.

At the Foot of the North Downs

We made our home in a little two up, two down end of terrace in Eccles Village, which nestles at the foot of the North Downs near Aylesford. We met a lot of special people there. As a family, we immersed ourselves in the surrounding countryside. We would walk around 'our circle,' have picnics and bike rides, mess about on the old rope swing someone else had set up by the stream, play 'bike he' and lots more. A wonderful place. When our children were old enough to be at home on their own, my husband and I enjoyed our lone romantic rambles.

Trees

If you've never hugged a tree, go out and do it now. And if you don't, ask yourself why. Trees give us life. To engage with Nature is liberating and invigorating. We happily handle small plants and shrubs, we hold bunches of flowers. Why not give a tree a great big hug? I dare you.

Change

When our first child was born, I had been so completely absorbed in the business of giving birth that it was only at the end, when our son was handed to us, that I realised how overwhelmed my young husband was. Our world had changed forever and Frank was awash with love, relief, pride and a great sense of responsibility. There were two student doctors present. The midwife asked one of them to take my blood. I recall he was shaking as he applied the syringe. The world changed for a few of us that day.

You Weren't Always This Big

I wrote this during a period of transition in my life and in the lives of my children. I wasn't needed any more in the way I had been used to. I wasn't the number one girl any more in the lives of my sons. To my daughter, I was just an annoyance who 'didn't understand.' It was true, I didn't and I should have tried harder to do so. It took me some time to realise that actually my husband and I must have done a reasonable job because our children were making their own way in the world and that's what any good parent wants.

Baby

Children are pure and innocent and wonderful. My children are grown up now but that raw, all consuming, fiercely protective love that sprang up the second I knew I was pregnant with them has never waned. It has been pulled and stretched, and tested and squeezed, but ultimately it is the same strong constant love. Yes, I have carried my children in every sense, and I always will when they need me to. And I know they will do the same for me now. When I need them to.

Limerick

Just a bit of fun with words. Wonderful words. The simplicity of the limerick belies the strict literary rules surrounding it. That is, it must be of five lines only with a rhyming pattern of AABBA.

Funny

More fun with words. The haiku originates from Japan and follows a strict literary pattern: seventeen syllables, arranged 5, 7, 5. I enjoyed breaking up the words in this one; it provides the brain with a little challenge and proves the marvel of that organ when processing language. We can still read it, can't we?

What You Mean to Me

I was inspired to write this poem by my children. As a parent, there is the possibility that we will become conceited and self congratulatory at what a good job we've done with our children. Hopefully, we give them all we can and we teach them all we can but there comes a time, if we are lucky, when we become aware of what they give us and what they teach us. Like love itself, the measure of these things is incalculable.

That Smile

This poem is for my grandson Thomas and for two year olds everywhere. We have all heard about the 'terrible twos' and yes, it is a real phenomenon. But that smile is irresistible, isn't it? That smile sends me a thousand messages: I am your son's son; I know I shouldn't really have this; please Nanny; thank you Nanny; I love you Nanny; whoops, I didn't mean to do that; I am your grand-son; may I have that; I know you love me Nanny...................... wonderful.

Night Watch

Love and Nature. Life depends on these two elements. The gibbous moon, the full moon, the crescent moon; she has featured in countless poems and stories. From the romance of the moonstruck lovers to the menace of the werewolf, the moon lives in our collective psyche. She is a major player on Nature's stage and I feel my connection to her. I look for the moon every night and I am disappointed if she is hidden by the clouds, though I know she is there; a constant presence in an uncertain life.

What Can I Do?

This poem is for my son who lost his daughter. When my child lost his little girl I couldn't make things better for him. I can help out in practical ways where I can. I will always listen to him and talk with him but I cannot make things better. I have a real faith, a real belief that Niamh is all right and we will see her again but the ache to hold her, to see her smile and to hear her never goes away. My son has had to be strong for the sake of his little boy. We must all carry on being strong, all of us together.

You

My inspiration for this poem is my granddaughter, Penny. I would walk forever to see her smiling face. She nurtures the child within me. She reminds me that everything is amazing. There is a connection between us no-one else can share. Then there is our shared connection with our family. She doesn't even need to be in the same place as me. Such is her magical power over me and the might of my imagination that I can see her face and feel her little body in my arms and life feels good.

Sports Day

I am a sensitive soul and my children's sports days stirred up a mixture of pride and anxiety within me. It didn't matter where they came in the race; I just willed them to get through it without falling over. I remember one time when my daughter tripped on her skipping rope. She picked herself up and bravely carried on, trying not to cry. Oh, but I wanted to cry. I did however enjoy the Mummys' race and I had the advantage of being the youngest mum there most years, which meant I usually won. My children loved that.

Not for Sale

There are people in the world who confuse love with ownership. This delusion is especially destructive when children are involved. One cannot own a living breathing person. That is not love. To retain the idea of owning another is the height of conceit and bordering on the psychopathic. Real love is about being there for someone without demanding conditions for one's support. It is about respect, consideration and knowing when to back off. One cannot own another and love cannot be bought.

My Cloak

After the loss of my granddaughter, people told me that it would change me and they were right. Life will never be the same as it was because she is no longer in this world with us. And I really do feel the physicality of my sadness. It is not all bad though because it is borne out of love. I want to mention here the staff at Cruse Bereavement Care in Maidstone, a charity providing a vital service to the bereaved. They helped me so much.

Another Springtime

For now, the spring has become a difficult time for me; all the new growth and the aliveness serves to remind me that my grand-daughter's young life was so tragically cut short. My consolation is the pink flowering cherry tree we planted in our garden in Niamh's memory. It assures me that her spirit lives and the tree is as beautiful as she was.

It Wouldn't Be the Same Without You

This poem is for all those people who are prepared to visit a theme park because everyone else in the group says it wouldn't be the same without them. We've all seen them, holding on to the coats and baggage. My husband is this person in our family. He'll happily go along 'for the atmosphere' but you will never persuade him to clamber onto one of the rides. I commend these people. And no, it wouldn't be the same without you.

Shopmania

Mad, mad, mad. Why do we do it? Why do we buy it? Why do we think we need it? I confess I'm attracted to anything pink and anything bright. Some years ago I was out shopping with my daughter. I had picked up something so insignificant and so obviously unnecessary that I have forgotten what it was. 'Put it

back, Mum,' said my daughter, 'you just want it because it's shiny.'
My cheeks still burn with shame.

Friends

Friends by definition are people one knows and trusts and friend-
ship is made on many different levels. From the friendship that
exists between different countries to that between colleagues at
work. From a lifelong friendship between adults to the transient
friendship shared between two infants who play with the toys
together at nursery school. All levels involve trust and respect to
some degree. We all know of sorry tales concerning the betrayal of
friends. I have learned lessons from my pretend friends. My true
friends enrich my life.

Moon

This is for my husband Frank and for moon lovers everywhere.
We were sixteen when we met at a disco. We married young then
had our three babies, along with an extended family of cats, dogs
and rabbits. One of the things that binds us together is our love
of Nature and the outdoors. I have a particular fascination with
the moon. And sometimes she is so bright, it really feels to me as
though I am looking at a mirror in the sky. What a miracle. She
gives me comfort and I know my loved ones in Heaven can see her
too.

Teacher

I wrote this for my teaching colleagues after completing my year's
employment as a Newly Qualified Teacher. Then I went on to
become a supply teacher, which presented its challenges, but gave
me great job satisfaction.

Tinnitus

I have been living with tinnitus and painful pressure in my ears for around thirteen years. Associated symptoms led to a diagnosis of possible Menieres disease. In the early days, I really thought the noise would drive me insane. I take medication to help combat the pain and pressure. When it's particularly loud, I wear hearing aids and sometimes I use a sound box at night which sounds like the ebb and flow of the tide. Silence is now a stranger to me and I miss it.

Ants

Automatic Negative Thoughts. That's a term I learned about when I first developed the problems with my ears. As I lay awake at two o'clock in the morning, feeling like I would be driven mad from the screaming noise in my head, getting to grips with my mental health became a matter of urgency. The ENT team at Medway Hospital has helped me a great deal and continues to support me. I still have difficult times but I cope better with them. I get up and read or write or complete a codeword. By applying my mind and relaxing, the ANTs recede.

Hello Sweetheart

We met our granddaughter for the first time on the day she was born. She arrived a few minutes after her twin brother, Thomas. Her little legs were purple and patchy after her forceps delivery. She was small, like her brother but she was healthy. Our daughter in law had not seen her babies since giving birth. My husband and I were so grateful that she and our son invited us to share that moment with them. Our granddaughter was named Niamh (Irish for radiance and brightness, pronounced Neeve.) Words can merely begin to express our joy at that time.

My love for my grandchildren is as great as my love for their parents; a different kind of love but every bit as great. And so it broke my heart when our son telephoned us from a London hospital to tell us that his little girl had passed away, overpowered by sepsis. Though I miss her so much I can ache, my spiritual and emotional connections with Niamh transcend the physical proximity, as with my children and my other grandchildren. If I say she died, I mean only that her little body expired, for my granddaughter's spirit lives in Heaven and Heaven is here on Earth if you look for it. If I say we lost her, I mean only that we lost the life we had with her. Niamh is not and never can be lost.

322 Days

We like to use the cliché in our wonderful language. Life is too short. You never know what's around the corner. Make the most of your time, you don't know how long you've got. Live each day as if it is your last. These phrases are so overused, the meanings are lost. I don't want to use these phrases any more. I now feel what they mean.

Goodbye Sweetheart

It is difficult to describe the pain of losing my grandchild. Her death was sudden and unexpected. I recall what fun we all had the last time we saw her. I remember thinking, 'I'll leave the camera in my bag – there will be lots of days like this.' I wanted to just experience and enjoy the moment. The next time I saw her, Niamh was at the undertakers wearing her best outfit and wrapped in her pink stripy blanket. We all know we were lucky to have had her at all. But saying goodbye to her killed me a little bit.

Things I Had Not Planned To Do

The first few days were full of practical needs. Our son and daughter in law needed looking after and so did their son. We also needed to support our other son and our daughter. Niamh's funeral needed arranging. As a family, we rallied and we gave her a beautiful day. We all knew it was the last Earthly thing we could do for her. That first Christmas was so hard. On New Year's Eve, my husband and I stayed up all night. We didn't want to go to sleep and leave that year behind because Niamh had been alive. And in the New Year she wasn't.

The Roar of The Sea

This poem works for me on three levels. There is the wonderful roar of the sea at Hythe in Kent, my favourite coastal vista. Then there is the roar of the tinnitus that lives in my head, which screams louder when I am disturbed in any way. Most powerful is the roar of my grief. In the first weeks after Niamh's passing, my husband could not leave the house. I couldn't bear to be inside so on this particular day I drove to Hythe on my own. I stood on the water's edge and I saw a distant white sail growing smaller and smaller. I imagined it to be my granddaughter and I cried.

A Rainbow from Heaven

My husband and I nurtured an awareness of Nature and the outdoors in our children and we do the same with our grandchildren. Just like Penny and Thomas do now, Niamh often went out in the garden with her Granddad and he would tell her the names of flowers and point out the birds and the butterflies. I remember early one morning showing her the blossom on the pear tree and watching as she touched it. Nature and children. How wonderful.

The Sky and All It Holds

Nature offers infinite inspiration for my writing. It is easily possible to go through a whole day without really looking at the sky. And the sky is a miracle, an endless expanse of wonder. It reminds me of my place in the world. It reminds me that I am not simply on this Earth, I am a part of it. So the sky is a part of me and mine to give to the people I love. Pass it on. Share it.

A Poem That I Wrote

I just love words, don't you? You can do what you want with them. I wrote this for a bit of fun for some friends. They had invited my husband and me to a New Year's Eve gathering where anyone could present a little performance if they wished to. A couple of other people recited poems and some sang folk songs to the accompaniment of various musical instruments. It was a memorable evening and a reminder of how special it is to have such nice people in our lives.

About The Author

I was born in a farm house on the edge of a cherry orchard in West Farleigh, Kent. My parents were farm workers and my early years were shaped by Nature and the countryside.

For as long as I can remember I have written; poems, stories, diaries, letters.

I attended a few schools as we moved around before arriving at Maidstone School for Girls. While studying for my A Levels, I met a boy who shyly asked me to dance at the Friday night disco at the Tudor House in Bearsted. That boy became my husband and we went on to have three children.

Life was busy but I always found time to learn new things. Reading and especially writing have always been integral to my life.

I worked in the nursery school attended by our children before going on to a primary school to support children with special educational needs.

I had a good set of O Levels and, after gaining a GCSE in mathematics and an A Level in English at my local college, I enrolled on a four year course at Christ Church University, Canterbury. I gained a 2:1(Hons) in English and Education along with a teaching qualification.

I went on to teach, becoming a supply teacher across all age ranges in local primary schools. When I developed problems with my ears, I gave up classroom teaching and taught English from home, helping young people struggling with their GCSE studies. Now, alongside my writing, I work as an administrator for my local Libraries, Registration and Archives Service.

Over the years I won a few prizes in newspapers and magazines; vouchers etc for my writing efforts. More recently I had a short piece featured in Prima magazine and a longer story published in the People's Friend popular summer annual.

Books have always featured in my life; they are my great friends. I have been inspired by too many writers and too many works to list them here but they include the wonderful story telling skills of Chaucer, Shakespeare, Austen and Dickens. I love the simplicity and honesty in the work of Wordsworth, particularly I Wandered Lonely as a Cloud and Composed Upon Westminster Bridge. I also enjoy the rawness of Thomas Hardy's work such as the poem The Darkling Thrush and his novel Far From the Madding Crowd. I can really relate to the anguished emotion of Alfred Lord Tennyson's Break, Break, Break.

I have put this anthology together for you. You will find I have a strong spiritual belief in God and the life beyond physical death. However, any ideas or opinions expressed on any topic are my own. I respect, indeed I celebrate our differences.

Apart from members of my own close family, no real person living or dead is featured in this collection; any perceived likeness is coincidence.

Finally, I truly hope you enjoy this collection and that you find at least one or two favourite poems you can revisit. I really enjoyed the writing process, though it was difficult at times and often very emotional. I gave my heart a spring clean and anything done for the sake of love is always worth doing.

Bridget Nolan 2017

Acknowledgements

Special thanks to my husband Frank for his love, his support and his encouragement.

Also to James Essinger of The Conrad Press for his guidance and advice and for turning this book into a reality. Thanks additionally to the cover designer and typesetter Charlotte Mouncey for her creative input and her patience.

And for everyone at The UK Sepsis Trust. www.sepsistrust.org